Lean Six Sigma

The Ultimate Guide to Lean Six Sigma, Lean Enterprise, and Lean Manufacturing, with Tools Included for Increased Efficiency and Higher Customer Satisfaction

© **Copyright 2018**

All rights reserved. No part of this book may be reproduced in any form without permission in writing from the author. Reviewers may quote brief passages in reviews.

Disclaimer: No part of this publication may be reproduced or transmitted in any form or by any means, mechanical or electronic, including photocopying or recording, or by any information storage and retrieval system, or transmitted by email without permission in writing from the publisher.

While all attempts have been made to verify the information provided in this publication, neither the author nor the publisher assumes any responsibility for errors, omissions or contrary interpretations of the subject matter herein.

This book is for entertainment purposes only. The views expressed are those of the author alone, and should not be taken as expert instruction or commands. The reader is responsible for his or her own actions.

Adherence to all applicable laws and regulations, including international, federal, state and local laws governing professional licensing, business practices, advertising and all other aspects of doing business in the US, Canada, UK or any other jurisdiction is the sole responsibility of the purchaser or reader.

Neither the author nor the publisher assumes any responsibility or liability whatsoever on the behalf of the purchaser or reader of these materials. Any perceived slight of any individual or organization is purely unintentional.

Contents

CHAPTER 1: UNDERSTANDING LEAN THINKING 8
    LEAN AND THE TPS APPROACH 10
    HOW TO USE THE HUMAN POTENTIAL 11

CHAPTER 2: THE BASICS OF SIX SIGMA 13
    HOW SIX SIGMA CAN WORK WITH THE LEAN PHILOSOPHY 13
    WHAT IS SIX SIGMA? 14
    WHY GO WITH SIX SIGMA? 14
    THE PHILOSOPHY OF SIX SIGMA 17
    TAKING ACTION 18

CHAPTER 3: WHAT IS LEAN SIX SIGMA? 19
    TOOLS OF SIX SIGMA 22
    WHY SHOULD I WORK WITH SIX SIGMA? 23
    THE PRINCIPLES OF LEAN 25

CHAPTER 4: PHASES OF LEAN SIX SIGMA 27
    PHASE 1: DEFINE 27
        Kano Analysis 28
    PHASE 2: MEASURE 29
        Project Charter 30
    PHASE 3: ANALYZE 30
        Hypothesis Testing 31
    PHASE 4: IMPROVE 31
        Solution Parameter 31
        Pilot Solution 31
    PHASE 5: CONTROL 32

CHAPTER 5: SYNTHESIZING LEAN AND SIX SIGMA 33

CHAPTER 6: PREPARING FOR LEAN SIX SIGMA ... 37
KNOWING YOUR CUSTOMERS ... 38
GROUPING THE CUSTOMERS ... 39
UNDERSTANDING THE CUSTOMER PROCESS ... 40
DEVELOP A HOSHIN PLAN ... 42
DEVELOP AN INFORMATION, PROCESS, AND INFRASTRUCTURE DIAGRAM ... 43

CHAPTER 7: UNDERSTANDING CUSTOMER NEEDS ... 44
THE KANO MODEL ... 44
IDENTIFYING YOUR CUSTOMER REQUIREMENTS ... 45
VOICE OF THE CUSTOMER ... 46
The Categories of VOC ... 47
VOC Methods ... 47
CUSTOMER ETHNOGRAPHY ... 49

CHAPTER 8: HOW TO GET TOP MANAGEMENT SUPPORT ... 51
STEALTH APPROACH ... 52
LIMITED INITIAL COMMITMENT APPROACH ... 53
HOW TO OVERCOME ANY RELUCTANCE TO LEAN SIX SIGMA ... 54

CHAPTER 9: DEPLOYMENT PLANNING ... 57
MAKING THE DECISION TO DEPLOY ... 57
CHOOSING A GOOD DEPLOYMENT MODEL ... 58
Organization-wide Model ... 59
Business Unit Model ... 59
Targeted Model ... 60
Grassroots Model ... 60
GETTING THE RIGHT TALENT ... 61
MAINTAINING FOCUS ... 61
IT IS WORTH IT? ... 62
DEPLOYMENT MISTAKES YOUR BUSINESS SHOULD AVOID ... 62
WEAK LEADERSHIP SUPPORT ... 62
TOO BROAD OF A SCOPE ... 63
POOR DEPLOYMENT STRATEGY ... 63
TOO MUCH EMPHASIS ON TRAINING AND CERTIFICATION ... 63
POOR PROJECT SELECTION ... 64
NOT PICKING OUT A DEPLOYMENT LEADER ... 65
ISOLATED IMPLEMENTATION ... 65

CHAPTER 10: PROJECT IDENTIFICATION AND SELECTION ... 66
IDENTIFYING, PRIORITIZING, AND SELECTING PROJECTS ... 69

CHAPTER 11: HOW TO SELECT A VIABLE DMAIC PROJECT ... 72

CRITICAL PROJECT CRITERIA 73

CHAPTER 12: VALUE ADDITION AND WASTE **76**

APPLYING WASTES TO TRANSACTIONAL PROCESSES 76
EXAMPLES OF WASTE PROBLEMS 77

CHAPTER 13: THE PROCESS-IMPROVEMENT TEAM **83**

THE DISADVANTAGE OF THE MANAGEMENT-LED PROCESS...............................84
THE BENEFITS OF THE TEAM-LED PROCESS 84
HOW TO CREATE A WINNING TEAM..85
HOW TO SELECT YOUR LEAN SIX SIGMA CANDIDATES 86
THE PROCESS OWNER 88

CHAPTER 14: DESIGN FOR LEAN SIX SIGMA **91**

DESIGN FOR SIX SIGMA..91
DESIGN FOR SIX SIGMA METHODOLOGY 92
HOW TO IMPLEMENT DESIGN FOR SIX SIGMA 93
THE BASICS OF DESIGN FOR SIX SIGMA 94

CONCLUSION..**98**

Chapter 1: Understanding Lean Thinking

The Lean philosophy is a set of practices, strategies, and methods specifically applied in business. This philosophy focuses on helping to improve the business and eliminate any waste that may be present. There's a popular belief that this model can only be used in the production industry or in manufacturing, but in truth, this is a concept that you can easily adapt to suit any type of business. It can help with handling different aspects of a company's operations such as consumer value, supply networks, and internal functions.

Different types of organizations could find that the Lean philosophy can have much to offer them. If they use it properly, it can provide rigorous methods to improve efficiency and reduce waste. While it may have started out being used in manufacturing, it has now become completely apparent that it can be used in almost all industries, including government, baking, retail, aerospace, healthcare, and construction, just to name a few.

The core aspect of the Lean philosophy is to try to reduce three main types of variation that show up in manufacturing. These variations are named *muda*, *mura*, and *muri*. Muda is a word from Japan that means "futility" or "uselessness". In business, this would refer to "waste". To help eliminate and reduce waste, the company needs to first separate activities that are considered value-adding from those that are needlessly costing the business money.

Mura can be defined as an "unevenness" in the business workflow processes. This kind of waste can sometimes cause needless downtimes or phases where there is a lot of unneeded strain on equipment, processes, and even employees. From a management standpoint, the unevenness is going to lead to a big challenge known as uncertainty. It is exceedingly difficult to plan for the future and run a business if the uncertainty levels are high. Any type of interruption that occurs in the workflow process can lead to the company's reduced ability to respond to customer needs. If the customer orders a product from the company and they have an expectation that the product will be delivered by a certain date, throwing some uncertainty into this mix can cause a lot of delays and chaos.

For a company to overcome mura, it needs to take serious considerations of its facilities, its assembly protocols, and how it does business. For most businesses, there needs to be a type of methodology for understanding processes better and for improving the ability to foresee potential problems.

Finally, muri refer to waste that resulted from the overburdening a system or from a deficient understanding of how that system works. If a business process or a production system starts to become overworked, it is possible that not only the machines but also the employees are going to suffer from wear and tear. Having a workload that is extremely high can result in a system failure and a high number of defective products.

When muri and mura combine, there is going to be a kind of bottleneck problem that would crop up in all parts of the organization. The best way to ensure that you are not straining the employees or the machines is to guarantee that your business is only focusing on the activities that add value. The company must also know how to minimize waste in other relevant areas to help reduce this kind of strain.

Another concept that comes with the Lean methodology – and can go hand in hand with reduction and identification of waste – is *kaizen*. This refers to "continuous improvement". It involves creating a culture inside your business where the group or the individual can choose to improve themselves as often as they want. This is a concept that almost all industries have begun to adopt.

The Lean philosophy incorporates many different tools, but the biggest factor that affects how it will impact the company is an attentive mindset. Everyone who is inside that company, from the CEO to the shop steward, need to be vigilant when it comes to eliminating waste, effecting changes that are positive, and continuously improving.

Lean and the TPS Approach

To get a better idea of how Lean thinking works, we need to look at the terms and tools that are used in the Japanese Toyota Production System. The TPS methodology is geared towards understanding how the processes work, figuring out methods to use to improve them, and then learning how to make the processes smoother and faster. If they end up discovering activities in the process that are not necessary, it is the job of the company to get rid of them.

However, if your company adopts the TPS approach, you need to realize that it is not a panacea for all the problems that you may be experiencing. This method is not all about the distinct elements – it puts the emphasis on how these elements are brought together to create a system that can be consistently put into practice each day. The principles need to be embedded into the thinking of all those in the organization, and there needs to be constant action and mindful implementation.

How to Use the Human Potential

No matter what kind of business you have, it is people that are going to form the core of your TPS approach. To get the results that you want, your employees need to be trained properly for them to adopt the beliefs and values that help bring about a stable and strong culture in your business. This means that you must constantly reinforce this new culture to ensure that it becomes a permanent feature.

In addition, each business needs to remember that people are the ones who create value. It is people who are going to implement the processes and use the equipment or the technology to make the project. To root out the waste from within, you need to first establish the right setting and culture for everyone to perform in.

In some situations, the Lean philosophy is going to be mistaken for a simple set of techniques and tools. However, you must remember that Lean is about the people first. There are a lot of companies who try to take the Lean methodology and use it, but they forget this one crucial point. This leads them to failure, and they suffer the consequences. The Lean method requires that everyone, from the highest levels to the lowest levels, change their mindset and then use the tools from the Lean methodology to reduce waste and improve the value presented to the customer.

This means that the company needs to know how to respect its people. It can do this by continually educating, training, challenging, and empowering them. Any organization that sees itself as "Lean" has to make sure that it sees its people as its most important asset. And as the most important asset, your people need to be celebrated, stimulated, and compensated properly.

That is one of the most important parts of the Lean methodology, especially when it comes to Lean Six Sigma. If the people of your company are not on board, then you are never going to see the successful completion of your project. It doesn't matter how much the management or owner or someone else wants Lean Six Sigma to work. If only a few people jump on board with enthusiasm, it is never going to work.

Once you can get everyone in the company on board with the idea of Lean Six Sigma and manage to help the right people get trained in the methodology, you'll increase your chances of being successful when you implement your projects. This guidebook will delve deep to explain the importance of getting everyone on board with Lean Six Sigma, and to show you some methods that you can use to ensure that everyone in your organization does so.

Chapter 2: The Basics of Six Sigma

How Six Sigma Can Work with the Lean Philosophy

Now that we know a little bit about the Lean philosophy, it is time to bring in an understanding of Six Sigma so you can see how these two things are going to combine to make a methodology that will really change the way that you can do business.

Businesses and organizations exist to serve their constituencies. These may include the shareholders and the owners of the company along with the customers who will purchase the products and services that are offered. Because of this, each organization and company need to find a way to create value. An efficient and effective organization must make sure that its output is greater than the input and that the value to be added will be created using minimal resources.

The whole purpose of working with Six Sigma is to enable the management to apply problem-solving and scientific principles to get the most value at a minimum cost. The technique involves being able to apply a methodology that is structured in order to improve any aspect of the business process that is already in existence. It is also there to help you design new products and processes with greater quality and performance.

What Is Six Sigma?

Six Sigma can be defined as a thorough, focused, and effective application of proven quality techniques and methodologies. This process aims to make sure you can eliminate every possible error and defect in the performance of a business. Sigma is the Greek letter used to measure variability.

The sigma level of the processes will measure the company's performance. In the past, most companies were content with sticking to a sigma level of three or four. Even at this level, the company would create tens of thousands of products that were defective per million opportunities. This is a high amount. Due to the customer expectations that have become higher in the past few years, Six Sigma had been set to have a standard of 3.4 problems per million opportunities.

The techniques and tools that Six Sigma can use will be applied with the help of a framework: a performance-improvement model referred to as DMAIC. These letters stand for:

- **D**: Define the goals of the activity that you will use to improve something in the business.
- **M**: Measure the system that you already have in place.
- **A**: Analyze the system to determine how to eliminate the gap between the current system/process performance and the end goal.
- **I**: Improve the system.
- **C**: Control the new system.

Why Go with Six Sigma?

During the 1970s, the Motorola plant that was in charge of manufacturing TV sets was taken over by a company from Japan. This new company decided that it was time to implement some big changes in the way the factory was being run. The new managers were able to get the factory to produce TV sets that had 1/20th as many defects than what the company had produced in the past.

The most surprising part about it was that these results were achieved with the same workers, designs, and technology as before. Additionally, the costs were reduced during the same time period. It became evident pretty early on that the main problem that had occurred with Motorola was the previous management that ran the factory.

The majority of people assume that the process of Six Sigma is only about quality because it is defined conventionally. Quality has traditionally been defined as "conformance to internal requirements." However, this is not the best type of definition of quality, and it is not going to give us a very accurate representation of what Six Sigma is actually about.

Six Sigma involves giving the organization a way to improve its process efficiency as well as its customer value in the hopes of increasing its profits. To link this objective with quality, a new definition has to be used.

When you apply the principles of Six Sigma, quality is going to be defined as "the value added by a productive endeavor." There are two main types of quality that we talk about here: potential and actual quality. With potential quality, we are referring to the maximum value that you can add to every unit of input. Actual quality, meanwhile, refers to the current value being added to every unit of input. The difference between these two is the waste.

The focus that comes with Six Sigma is that you want to use it to eliminate waste and to improve the quality of products and services inside a company. Unlike a lot of cost-cutting programs that some businesses like to work on, Six Sigma is not trying to reduce both the quality and the value of the products and services that you provide in the hopes of cutting down your expenses; it takes a different route. It places emphasis on identifying and then eliminating any costs that don't end up adding value to customers even when the quality of the product is improved.

Most companies are willing to sacrifice the quality so that they can reduce their costs and make more money. But this is not a good method to go with if your company wants to keep customers around and make more money. Six Sigma doesn't follow this form of thinking either. It is going to spend its time focusing on customer needs, preventing defects, reducing the cycle time, and helping the customer save a lot on costs.

Now, it is important to understand the sigma level as well – it is going to be directly related to the quality level. As we described earlier, a Six Sigma company is going to fail to achieve its requirements about three times out of every million transactions. When we look at an average company, usually classified as a four sigma, they are going to fail to meet the quality requirements about 6,210 times for a million transactions. Think of what a difference this is in waste, customer satisfaction, and more!

Studies have also shown that the companies who are at a four sigma are more likely to experience high operating costs, mostly because 25 to 40 percent of their revenue is going to be used to help fix problems.

On the other hand, companies who use Six Sigma and are successful with it can spend just five percent, if not less, of their revenues on fixing problems that come up. This gap is known as the cost of poor quality, and research has shown that the gap costs four sigma companies about ten billion dollars total each year. You can see why implementing Six Sigma can be a great way to ensure that you keep your costs down while still providing a great product or service to your customers.

One of the questions that your business should always ask is "Why is it necessary to relate costs to sigma levels?" To keep things simple, sigma levels are there to indicate error rates, and as every person in business knows, spending time on fixing errors will cost money.

As your sigma level starts to go up, the error rates and your operating costs will start to drop sharply. The truth is that in the modern business world, nobody wants to tolerate lots of errors and defects when they are working on producing their product or service because this can cost the company a lot of money.

The Philosophy of Six Sigma

To implement Six Sigma, you will need to work with several scientific methods to help design and operate your business management systems and processes. This is done to help your employees provide more value to both the shareholders and your customers. A good example of the scientific method as it is used with Six Sigma is the following:

>1. A critical part of the market or the business will be identified.
>2. Once this aspect is found, you form a hypothesis that is consistent with your observation.
>3. You make some predictions based on the hypothesis that is formed.
>4. Experiments are then conducted to test out the predictions that you made. Based on the new data that you collected, you may have to make some changes to the hypothesis. If there are any variations, you would then need to use some statistical tools to help distinguish between noise and signal.
>5. Repeat steps three and four until there are no longer any discrepancies between the hypothesis and the actual results that you get.

While this is a simple version of the method that you go through when using Six Sigma, it is very effective. If you use this method for a longer period of time, your company is then going to be able to develop a viable theory that will make it easier for you to understand your business processes as well as your customers.

In reality, many companies are going to make big important decisions, but they will not be able to provide hard data to explain some of these decisions. However, if they use the scientific method like we just talked about above and they continuously implement it, it is going to create a fundamental attitude shift that will cause management to question whether what they know can match up with what the data shows.

The point of this philosophy is to shift everyone's focus to the company's stakeholders: the customers and the owners. If the processes, as well as the management systems of a company, are designed properly, and they are run by employees who are happy, then your stakeholders will be happy.

The trouble here is that many traditional companies believe that they actually do this when in reality, they don't. The big difference is that a company that uses Six Sigma is going to take a more rigorous and systematic approach when they implement this new philosophy.

Taking Action

The world of business is going to move very quickly. This means that a company that plans to implement Six Sigma is not going to have the luxury of spending years to research a problem before they come up with the decision that they want to use. For the management in one of these companies, it is critical to determine how much information they will find useful enough to take the course of action that they want.

Once the management is confident that they have enough information to make a decision, then the project will be able to move from the Analyze phase they were just in over to the Improve stage or from the Improve phase over to the Control stage. Though the company would have discovered many more opportunities if it were able to spend more of its time looking over the information, they are still going to come up with fewer mistakes compared to a company that doesn't use the techniques of Six Sigma at all.

Chapter 3: What Is Lean Six Sigma?

Lean Six Sigma has its origin in the concept of Six Sigma. The Six Sigma philosophy can be traced back to the mid-eighties when American production companies needed a method to change their production style and compete with the prevailing, and superior, Japanese production styles. Six Sigma was what resulted – a methodology by which companies could easily and effectively remove waste from their manufacturing process.

Lean Six Sigma, specifically, is based on the integration of Six Sigma with Lean Manufacturing and Lean Enterprise. In essence, it takes concepts from both and weaves them into a single system. The entire point of Lean Six Sigma is to massively reduce the amount of waste that occurs in the manufacturing of products. To break down its two components, the Lean aspect is focused on breaking the production process down such that the maximum possible amount of manufacturing waste is eliminated. If you recall, these wastes are referred to as *muda*, and they can be collectively remembered through the acronym DOWNTIME. We'll be going into that in just a moment.

Meanwhile, the Six Sigma component is based around the utilization of five key processes or phrases referred to as DMAIC, which will be covered specifically in the next chapter. These phases are intended to help with the general analysis of workflows and business processes to improve them in such a way that the end goal of the process is achieved in a more meaningful and predictable manner. Six Sigma is particularly focused on the implementation of data analysis technologies to come to meaningful conclusions regarding the business processes and best practices within all relevant realms.

Now, bearing all of that in mind, let's take a second to analyze the different kinds of waste that Lean Six Sigma aims to eliminate through the implementation of various practices.

Waste has been defined as anything other than what is absolutely needed for a business to make as much profit as possible. Waste, therefore, counts as anything additional that takes away from the product – buying too much equipment or too many parts, overuse of those things beyond their maximum profit potential, and any additional labor beyond what is needed to generate the most profit possible.

The Lean system defines eight different kinds of waste.

The first major kind of waste is named Defects. The idea of Defects refers to the need to get rid of any given products because a component or the product itself is defective. The Lean Six Sigma system aims to analyze where and how these defects are occurring to minimize them.

After Defects comes the concept of Overproduction. Overproduction refers to making more of a product than the amount that can be bought and consumed. This creates waste in numerous different ways. Firstly, it means that the business is wasting resources, monetary or otherwise, on things which ultimately are only going to hurt their profit margin. Moreover, the products will eventually become trash or might be bought at a far lower price than the value they were intended to be sold at, meaning that the company takes a loss while hurting the environment in the process. When it comes to Overproduction, the producer also needs to understand that customer needs and, more importantly, market forces, are dynamic.

The next major kind of waste is the concept of Waiting. Waiting refers to any sort of downtime within the company where labor is being paid for but isn't being utilized. Another example is when a product is sitting, waiting to be processed or to be shipped. As an example, let's say a company has a product shell that needs final processing. Instead of getting to it, however, the company spends an excessive amount of time allowing that product to sit on the shelf, just waiting to be processed further.

Next comes the extremely important concept of Neglect (also called *Defect* or *Unused Talents*). Neglect refers to how a company could literally neglect to use all of the skills that its workers have to offer or else fail to allow the workers to give each other and the upper management the ability to share information and learn from one another. Instead, tasks are delegated in a very hierarchical way, and there is a stubborn refusal to allow the rigid roles that workers fill to change in any way, shape, or form.

After Neglect is Transportation. Transportation refers to the fact that any time a thing is transported from one location to another, the company runs the risk of that product being lost or damaged or having its release rate and shipment date come under delay – or both. In addition, the process of transportation adds to the cost of the product, but it fails to generate any sort of value to the product itself.

Let us now talk about Inventory. Inventory refers to any unfinished resource or product from a resource that hasn't been turned into its final sellable form yet and is therefore only taking up vital space resources. It is generating company waste by wasting labor hours as well as by taking up physical space that could be used for something else. Maintaining a steady workflow will allow for this to be mitigated as much as possible, ensuring that products and resources aren't just sitting around waiting to be completed.

The penultimate letter in our acronym stands for Motion. The concept of Motion stands in parallel to the concept of Transportation. While they both reference one thing or another, the motion waste category refers to any sort of negative effects or damage which are incurred on the resources that actually generate the product. In essence, if the laborers are getting hurt or if the machines are breaking down over time due to repeated use, this could be considered a form of motion waste. Motion also refers to any time that the machines need to be shut down or the workers must be allowed to take time off due to the maintenance of the damage.

The last major kind of waste is Excess (also called Extra-Processing). Excess refers to the idea of doing things to a product that, while adding more value, the consumer of the product ultimately doesn't need or want. This means that the company wastes money and resources on additional features that are ultimately unappreciated or useless.

These concepts that form the acronym DOWNTIME are the major forms of waste that the Lean Six Sigma system aims to reduce or completely get rid of. Lean Manufacturing and Lean Enterprise are specifically geared toward eliminating these forms of waste.

The Six Sigma system integrates extremely well with the Lean system; it's almost synergistic, in fact. Where Lean Manufacturing is focused around waste, Six Sigma puts emphasis on incremental processes and data analysis to curb said waste and ensure that the company is moving along as smoothly as possible.

Tools of Six Sigma

There are a lot of different tools that are at your disposal when working with Six Sigma. Some of the key ones that you may want to use when implementing Lean Six Sigma into your business include the following:

- Statistical process control

- Voice of the customer
- Process design
- Root cause analysis
- Process management
- Balanced Scorecards
- Business process management
- Change management
- Continuous improvement

Six Sigma is a great methodology to use that will ensure that you can get your defect rates down to as little as possible while reducing waste. When you can add it together with the Lean philosophy, you will find that your business is going to reach a whole new level and will be better equipped to handle the business world and gain a competitive edge.

Why should I work with Six Sigma?

If your business is thriving and doing pretty well, why would you want to apply some of the methods of Six Sigma? Why do so many different businesses adopt this approach? While some companies that have tested out this system did not achieve their overall goals, those who had applied this approach using the right tools and methods did see some results. There are quite a few benefits that come with implementing Six Sigma, and these are as follows:

- It can help strengthen the business and will boost the chances of the company surviving and succeeding. Six Sigma can provide the tools that are needed to change and innovate with the market, making success more attainable.

- It gets everyone working to the same performance goal. No matter the size of the company, working to make sure that all employees work towards one common goal can be difficult. Since every unit in your company is going to have its own objectives to work towards, the only thread that is common is the delivery of services, products, and information to the customer. By focusing on the process and the customers, Six Sigma can develop a consistent goal and an almost perfect level of performance.

• It prioritizes value for the customers. Many companies that use this methodology say that it has helped improve their perspective of what value means to the customers. Even though a company may already hold the title of being the best in the field, performance is still often far removed from what the customer expects. Six Sigma enables the company to focus on delivering a good value to the customer while still earning a profit.

• It can book performance and can improve the rate of improvement. No organization doesn't have the goal of improving each day, but most fail at it. Six Sigma gives a company the ability to adopt tools and concepts from a wide variety of disciplines to help establish a foundation that accelerates performance and improvement.

• It can create a company that learns. When your employees constantly learn, it means that you are going to get more ideas out of them, and this can push you into the future.

The Principles of Lean

While we will spend more time talking about these principles later on, as we move through this guidebook, it is important to get a good understanding of the Lean philosophy before you get started with Lean Six Sigma. To implement this philosophy in your company, you must consider these five principles ahead of time:

1. Start out by specifying the value of the product, but look at it from the perspective of your end consumer. Value is going to be defined by the customer and not by the company. It doesn't matter what you think of the product. If the customer doesn't like it, they are not going to purchase it. It is necessary for you, as a company, to understand your processes, improve the flow, and prevent waste as much as possible.

2. Determine the steps in your value stream for your product or a particular family of products. Once you have all the steps in front of you, it is easier to see which of them aren't adding any value and are just wasting time.

3. Ensure that the steps that remain are ones that are necessary and will add some value to the process. Additionally, make sure that these steps are in a tight sequence. This ensures that the product will be able to flow smoothly, without extra waste or costs, straight to the customer.

4. Once your flow is established, and you are sure that the unneeded steps have been eliminated, you can allow the customers to pull value from your new processes.

5. Start this process all over again. You will want to keep going through these steps on repeat until you come close to perfection.

Lean thinking exists to provide your company with an effective way to enhance the amount of value your customers can receive by eliminating the wastes and ironing the process flow.

Chapter 4: Phases of Lean Six Sigma

This chapter focuses on the specific phases of Lean Six Sigma and their individual goals. As addressed in the previous chapter, the Six Sigma process is based around a five-phase system known as DMAIC. DMAIC is short for Define, Measure, Analyze, Improve, and Control. This chapter is going to break all of this down so that you can form a better understanding of what all of these phases are intended to do and what they provide to the user.

Phase 1: Define

The Define phase is based around the simple goal of understanding what the end goal of the process is regarding company and workflow revision measures. The first essential part of this is learning what your problem is. Since Lean Six Sigma is based around managing your production and refining your overall process of production, you need to define your problem first and foremost – and your problem is your method of production. Somewhere along the line, you are being wasteful in your production methodology. You might be spending too much on unnecessary things, or you might just be wasting money where you don't need to. This part of the process is about understanding what that problem is and then defining clear-cut goals for the entire process.

Kano Analysis

The idea of Kano Analysis is about looking at either your product or your production process and trying to find places where cutbacks can be made. Essentially, you're outlining the requirements of the product and/or the production process and then breaking them down into five different groups: basic requirements, which are the things that you absolutely must be doing; performance requirements, which are the things that actually help to improve end-satisfaction for the final recipient of the product; indifferent requirements, or things that will neither help nor hurt the end-satisfaction of the recipient and are therefore not necessary; reverse requirements, which are things that can actually hurt you if they're fulfilled; and delighter requirements, which are things that are meant to attract people to a given product, even if they aren't necessarily needed for the product or for the production process to run as intended. Again, these can either refer to the end-satisfaction of the customer with the process or the overall running status of the production process.

The Define phase is going to be the first one you will work with in Lean Six Sigma. The leaders of the project will come up with a project charter that they want to work with. They will then develop a high-level view of the process and then move on to understanding the needs of the customers. The team needs to create an outline they can use to guide all of their efforts. This outline should include a few important things like defining the problem, the goals, the process, and the customer.

When defining a problem, you must come up with a problem statement. There should be data that shows this problem already exists inside a process. Then, the team should verify that this problem is of high priority and that, if it is not resolved, it is going to have a big impact on the company. Finally, they need to ascertain whether the company has enough resources to solve the issue.

Defining the problem statement involves defining measurable and time-bound terms of what the project success will look like. Taking the time to define a process can be done by making maps to help your team decide which areas are the most critical and should be looked into. Defining the customer and all their needs will involve contacting at least some of these customers to hear what they have to say. This will provide your team with information that can be very useful for solving your problems.

Phase 2: Measure

The Measure phase revolves around obtaining current metrics regarding production and waste for you to have something concrete to build on. It will help you gain an idea of where you need to be developing from and where your baseline is. This is one of the most critical points in the whole process.

This step is where you quantify the problem. It is important that you constantly measure the process with the team leaders who ought to focus on the collection of data. The first step here is to establish the current performance of your process or the baseline that you can use to measure how things are going. You want to have this baseline in place before you make any major changes.

The second step is for you to determine the cause of the waste or the problem with the help of the data you collected. The team must be able to create a very detailed plan to collect data, and it should include where they will get the data, how much they should collect, and who will be responsible for this task. Make sure that your team can collect data they find reliable rather than making assumptions.

Finally, the team needs to be able to update the project charter. By the time they are done with the measuring phase, there should be a lot of information about the process performance, goals, and problems.

Project Charter

The project charter can immensely help you develop an idea of what is necessary for the next steps. The project charter is composed of five aspects. The first aspect is the business case, which outlines why the project in question is important; in the Lean Six Sigma context, this has to do with ensuring that waste is cut. The second aspect is the statement of both the problem faced and the end goal of the entire project. The third is the project scope, which defines what the project covers and, ideally, what things define the end of the project. The fourth is the project milestones, which clarifies when different tasks need to be completed in the context of the project. Last is the delegation of resources and roles, where you define what you'll need and what everyone will be doing.

Phase 3: Analyze

During the Analysis period, you're trying to determine reasons for the hitches in your process and what the root causes of those problems are. This process involves having your team identify the root cause of the problem. It is your team's job to collect the data, and you can go ahead and split this up according to the types of data that you need to pour over. The review team will have taken the time to analyze the data collected during your Measure phase, and they can choose whether or not they want to be able to include more information in here. The aim in this step is to find the root causes of all your waste and defects.

During this phase, it is important for you to inspect each step of the process with the help of a Process Analysis. The team should be able to brainstorm all the probable causes of the waste, the defects, and the time that is lost. Before you end this step and move on to your Improve phase, the causes of your problem need to be double-checked. Once the additional data is obtained, you can then update the project charter.

Hypothesis Testing

In the Analysis process, you're going to be doing what's called hypothesis testing. What hypothesis testing essentially means is coming up with different reasons for why one thing or another is happening. If possible, you're going to try to force a statistical measure of comparison between the two by measuring the likelihood of one error or the other would take place. You're going to be compressing your comparisons into one singular root cause that you can then endeavor to fix.

Phase 4: Improve

During the Improve period, you're dedicated to coming up with a solution for the problem or problems identified in the last phase of the DMAIC process. You're trying to ultimately come up with some sort of meaningful solution, then implementing that solution over time through a strategically implemented plan of action.

Solution Parameter

In the solution parameter method, you will be attempting to name different solutions and then come up with parameters for each. These parameters should be answering essential questions such as how each solution is superior to the others. Afterward, come up with numerous solutions and then write a decision statement which outlines all of the different things that a given solution absolutely needs to meet.

Afterward, start to sort your criteria into two different categories: the things which must happen and the things that you want to happen. When a solution doesn't satisfy the first category, the team knows that it isn't a suitable solution. The team can then use the second category to decide on a given solution.

Pilot Solution

Afterward, you need to actually try implementing the solution in question and seeing how it fares. If the results come out positive, then you know that the solution is worthwhile and you can try to adapt it to a much larger scale.

Phase 5: Control

The last phase is the Control phase, which is based around monitoring the implemented changes over a longer period of time and ensuring that the changes are worthwhile and that they continue to work. This phase also aims to make sure that there is an appropriate infrastructure in place to help guarantee that the same problems won't arise again and that the solutions work effectively over the long term. Over time, watch your solution and its various metrics to be certain that it's moving along as you hoped it would; this will give you an important frame of reference for long-term implementation and maintenance.

The point of this stage is to sustain the new solution that you've put in place. It is similar to what you see in process management, and the team that is involved is going to spend time documenting how the employees within this process will access and then utilize their new infrastructure. Keep in mind that this process must always be worked on and improved and that the control is never a one-off event.

What this means is that the team in charge of figuring out and developing new solutions must identify a few parameters that they should monitor throughout, and this should also go hand in hand with a response plan in case any problems arise. There should be plenty of ways to document the process, including using process maps and checklists. The new knowledge gained will then be used to improve processes in other parts of the company. Of course, every project that was successful should be shared and celebrated with everyone.

Chapter 5: Synthesizing Lean and Six Sigma

As you can see, there are many steps to the Six Sigma process, but it's not as complicated as it might appear. The Six Sigma process and the Lean ideal actually work together extremely well, allowing you to massively reduce the waste of your entire workflow. Specifically, through the data analysis of Lean Sigma as well as the measurement phase, you'll be able to find places in your process that need to be improved upon.

You will then be able to use the Lean Sigma Six methodologies systematically to come up with a large number of solutions. These solutions have a great potential to improve your production holistically. The best way to implement the two together would be to start from the very top, with the more general issues regarding your production process and where things are going awry.

If you find that, for example, you're wasting a lot of time waiting, then you should ideally try to find a way that you can eliminate as much of said type of waste as possible. Then, you should work your way down, finding less and less general problems as you fine-tune your production process and try to eliminate as many different sources of waste as you can. Lean Six Sigma is designed to help you understand why and how your company is creating waste, and it gives you the tools and framework to try to fix it yourself.

All companies have the same goal in mind when it comes to running their business. They want to produce a product as cheaply as possible and deliver it to the customer as quickly as they can, and they want to do it with as few impediments and challenges as possible.

The weak link with this change is also the potentially strongest link: people. Each company needs to have a lot of people to help it run. They need those who make the product, those who send the product out to customers, those who answer questions, those who help the customers, those who market, and so much more. If the people know how to do their jobs and are willing to work together, they become a strong link for the company; however, if the company doesn't have people who can work together, especially with lots of different departments, a lot of waste could result.

To ensure that you are increasing how productive people are to minimize some of your risk and your waste, you will want to turn to a process that works. The Lean process was originally developed by the Toyota Company. They decided that they were wasting a lot of time and money in their manufacturing plants and decided to make changes to decrease all this waste. The changes ended up increasing how efficient the Toyota Company was.

Since that time, the Lean production philosophies have gone into many different businesses and helped them remove waste and do better at business. While it was originally developed as a manufacturing tool, it has found its way into many different types of businesses as well as into many industries and shops. Lean thinking can even be found in many different industries such as software houses.

As Toyota was working on developing the Lean philosophy, Motorola was doing something similar with their Six Sigma methodology. This methodology found wide acclaim during the

1990s when General Electric, with the help of their leader Jack Welch, developed one cornerstone of the business. These two companies ended up needing to accomplish the same thing. They wanted to be able to combine the efficiency of their people with their requirement to cut down waste. The two concepts are now linked. They share a lot of similarities, and most companies will choose to go with the Lean Six Sigma approach rather than use them separately.

While Six Sigma focuses on improving the process of a business with the help of a statistical analysis of production metrics, the Lean methodology focuses on improving the flow of the business and then eliminating any area of the process that is disruptive and uneven. These can be as simple as having tools or other items in awkward positions, having a workstation that is disorganized, or having clutter that tires the body and the mind.

Each business will have to decide how they want to make these improvements. By having a team in place that looks over all the places in the business that need improvements and then prioritizing what needs to be done first, they'll be sure to pick out projects that will provide them with the biggest benefits.

Like many other business terms, the concept of flow can cross through a variety of boundaries. Professional programmers, athletes, and artists are all looking to get into a state that is known as being "in the zone". These manufacturing techniques and processes will make it easier for your employees to be as effective as possible while enjoying satisfying working conditions at the same time.

While most of Six Sigma is mostly about statistics, Lean is going to be more about the flow of the work. But despite these differences, they have people in common. If you can get people to be a part of the process the right way and from the beginning, the rest is going to follow.

Some theories state how using Six Sigma and Lean together seem to be counterintuitive, but they do work well as one entity despite that.

This is because when you combine them, they are both able to make positive financial improvements to an organization through a good return on investment.

The main point here is that you need to be able to use Six Sigma and the Lean methodology together. To achieve the operational excellence that you are looking to gain, don't treat them as separate entities or processes.

When you use the Lean methodology and Six Sigma, you will learn how to focus on purpose, people, and process. This allows you to achieve a better value stream that will end up delivering the highest value to your customer, the highest quality that you can produce, and the lowest cost to the business. It is going to give you a competitive advantage over others, as long as you use it in the proper manner, and it will give you the differentiation that your company may be requiring right now.

Many companies might be exploring different options that they can use to reduce the waste in their companies and become more efficient. They know that this is going to help them provide better customer service, make a better product, and even save a lot of money. The good news is that when you are considering whether to go with the Lean methodology or with Six Sigma, you can combine these two into the Lean Six Sigma methodology and get amazing results.

Chapter 6: Preparing for Lean Six Sigma

Now that you know a little bit more about Lean Six Sigma, it is time to prepare to implement it. Many of the companies decide not to go with Lean Six Sigma because they think that the methods are just too complex. They claim that they simply do not have the right resources to develop an infrastructure and then train the employees as needed. These companies can even go to the extent of saying that this method is a burden that would actually end up weighing them down further, making it next to impossible to meet the needs of their customers.

Companies that say such things usually don't have a clear understanding of how Lean Six Sigma works. Sure, it does take some time to train your employees to get them ready to use it, but this methodology is there to make you more efficient, to help you provide better customer service, and so much more. Let's take a look at some of the things that you need to do to get prepared for Lean Six Sigma; that is, getting to know more about your customers so you can serve them better.

Knowing Your Customers

The first thing that you will need to do to prepare for Lean Six Sigma is learning who your customers really are. You will find that knowing your customer is going to make all the difference when it is time to prepare for your Lean Six Sigma project. If you spend all your time trying to make changes to a product or a process while not giving any consideration to how your customer will like the changes or how these changes are going to affect them, then you are going to waste a lot of your own time and money.

There are going to be three critical factors that you must consider to determine your true customers and how you can help them best. These three factors are listed below:

> 1. *The primary customer*: Many companies fall into the trap of thinking that their distributor is their primary customer. But this is not true. The end-consumer has needs and requirements that you must take care of. If you don't do this, you are going to suffer because the demands for your services and products will drop.
>
> ➤ Of course, you can still consider the distributor as a type of customer. Your distributor is very crucial to the process because they are the one who pushes the product for you. However, the thing to remember is that if the end-customer is happy, the distributor is also going to benefit.
>
> 2. *The congruency of the pain points of different customers*: Your customers may have needs that are similar, but there will also be needs that are not congruent. It is your job to understand where these differences and similarities in pain points lie.
>
> ➤ For example, a dealer may be more interested in efficient transactions while the end-user will need more guidance and education. These two pain points are

distinct, and the company might need to address both or just one. The company could measure out the impact of each of these pain points on its revenue stream and figure out which one is more important.

3. *The worth of the customer*: It is true that one end-user can't be equal to one distributor or one dealer. On the other hand, your dealer is only going to be happy if the end-user is happy. An end-user who is not happy with the services and products of the company could cost the dealer time and money.

➤ If this gets bad enough, a dealer who sells several different brands may be forced to recommend rival brands over yours. This is a big financial loss for you as a company, especially over the long term. You need to ask yourself which customers have the greatest worth for you.

Grouping the Customers

A good way for you to look at your customers and see their different requirements is to segment them out into groups. This is useful for developing products and services that will meet the distinct requirements of each group. It can also enable the company to develop measures that can address performance issues relating to each group.

It is important that you take the time to group your customers together. There are often so many customers that it becomes nearly impossible for you to consider them all and try to figure out what they will want if you look at them as a whole. However, when you take the time to group your customers, you are more likely to find useful patterns. Plus, this is a great way for you to get a better feel for your customers and what they want and need from your products, services, and business.

You can group your customers in any manner that you choose, but some of the options that you can consider include:

- Age
- Size
- End use
- Price sensitivity
- Spend
- Socio-economic factors
- Impact
- Buying characteristics
- Industry
- Frequency of purchase
- Loyalty
- Geographical location
- Gender

Understanding the Customer Process

The first thing that you need to do to develop an organized approach to understanding your customer process is to create a customer strategy. Most companies may feel that their customer strategy is pretty solid; i.e., allotting a large budget for the sales department. However, that is an example of a weak customer strategy that won't really help you understand how the customer process works. So what will be the best approach to take to help you understand the customer process?

There are three different ways that team leaders and managers can outline and then document the customer strategy for a business. Some of these are as follows:

Developing a Business Architecture

This step aims to ensure that everyone in the company can visualize and understand the different departments and how they are linked. The problem with most traditional companies is that the workers have no idea how the activities they do each day will affect the other departments. Depending on which department they are in, they may not even understand how their work is affecting the customer. For a Lean Six Sigma company, an understanding of business architecture will help to resolve this issue.

To understand business architecture people need to be able to view it graphically. You will need to represent it on a diagram that can easily present how your customers are linked to the different business processes. Remember that these processes are not going to be the same thing among the departments inside the company.

To make things a bit easier, there are five key things that can help you determine if a company has developed a functional business architecture. These include the following:

- The architecture is simple enough that it can fit into a one-page diagram.
- Each department inside the company is represented in the diagram.
- The architecture can link together the departments relative to the processes that your customers care the most about.
- Each person in the company will be able to draw a line of sight from the work they accomplish each day to the customer.
- The architecture focuses more on how the company plans to satisfy customer needs so that it can achieve its goals rather than on how the business is currently being run.

Developing this kind of business architecture is going to make it easier for other work processes to flow. Once you have it in place, customer research is more easily steered in the right direction. For example, products can be evaluated to help determine how effectively they can provide value to the customer, or funds can be channeled toward the processes that need it the most. Measures that solve problems can be refined to suit this architecture as well.

Develop a Hoshin Plan

Hoshin is a word that can be translated to mean compass. This is a strategic planning process that will involve the company setting its direction and then aligning available resources to help meet long-term goals. Hoshin planning involves executing and formulating strategies to help you meet the needs of your company while also attaining the goals of shareholders. It is going to document the approach and the 12-month performance plan of your organization. A Hoshin plan should include the following elements:

Deploying objectives

- Establish key metrics at the executive level.
- Decide on the operational, financial, and customer metrics to help support your strategic metrics.
- Narrow down the key metrics so that you can focus on the ones that are the most critical.
- Agree on how these measures are taken and how they will be reported.
- Review the performance each week.

Selecting the key projects

- Ensure that all the key projects can be linked back to your Hoshin plan.
- Ensure that a project isn't chosen just because it is a cost-avoidance measure. Every project needs to show evidence of bringing about improvement in productivity, customer delight, and income saves.
- Review the project at an executive level. This can be done each month to help determine what progress has been made toward the objectives.
- Focus on measurable progress during the reviews and ensure that the right financial resources are available ahead of time.

- Celebrate the success of a completed project and move on to the next one.

Develop an Information, Process, and Infrastructure Diagram

The role of the IPI diagram is to elevate the business architecture and the Hoshin planning strategies by painting an accurate picture of the present as well as the future business environment. This diagram is created through a process that strives to be both iterative and dynamic. The common practice is to use the DMAIC tools to help you get the right documentation and information. You will then create the drawings and, finally, verify these drawings to make sure that they are doing a good job of representing the present and future environment of the company.

One of the foundational elements that you will find in an IPI diagram is the SIPOC, or the Supplier, Input, Process, Output, and Customer diagram. This diagram should depict what an organization does to meet the needs of a customer.

Another building block of this diagram is the value stream map. This one is going to help you know which steps will add value, and which ones won't while looking from the perspective of your customer.

A customer strategy process that is well-defined should be supported by the IPI diagram, the Hoshin plan, and the business architecture. A customer-centric company should always strive to enhance the experience of the customer while also being able to generate more profits and accelerate growth.

All of these parts are needed to help the business use the Lean Six Sigma method the right way. Without understanding your customer properly, all the strategies that you work on are going to fall short. Take a look at the information you have about your customer, as well as some of the sections talked about in this chapter so that you can get ready to work with Lean Six Sigma.

Chapter 7: Understanding Customer Needs

The needs of your customer are always changing. Some of the services or products that people thought were useful a few years ago are no longer on the market. In some cases, the customer may not even realize that their needs have changed, and they will be surprised, in a good way, when the business comes up with new and more advanced products to use. Let's take a look at some of the measurement techniques that you can use to gain a deeper understanding of your customer.

The Kano Model

The Kano analysis can help a company analyze the needs of the customer and how it can identify these requirements. According to this model, customer satisfaction is going to be proportional to the level of functionality that the service or product has. The Kano model is going to focus on satisfying three types of needs:

- *Basic needs*: You must be able to satisfy basic needs just to enter the market. These basic needs are the expected characteristics that a service or product has. They are not usually spoken of because they are pretty obvious. If these basic needs are not met, the customer is going to be extremely dissatisfied. For example, a clean table and clean silverware are considered basic needs at a restaurant. The customer will expect these without asking.

• *Performance needs*: Satisfying these needs allow the company to keep themselves on the market. Performance needs are going to be the standard features that will either reduce or elevate the satisfaction of the customer, depending on their scale, such as the speed or the price. These needs are typically asked for by the customer. Going back to the restaurant example, these could include the customer asking for a non-smoking section or Wi-Fi access.

• *Excitement needs*: When you satisfy these needs, you can move up to be a world-class company. The products or services should include some features that, while unexpected, will impress the customers. These are not usually asked for. For example, a hotel could provide fresh baked cookies during turndown service.

Identifying Your Customer Requirements

Basic customer needs can be identified in several ways. The best techniques that you can use to help you out with this include the following:

- The win and loss reports
- Internal quality process measures
- Attrition analysis
- Complain systems

You can also take the time to identify performance needs. You can identify these using the following techniques:

- Focus groups
- Surveys on customer satisfaction

- Perceptual surveys
- Transactional reports

In addition, you will need to look at some of the excitements needs. To determine what these are, use the following techniques:

- Leading edge forums
- Invent-the-future focus programs
- Customer loyalty programs

The Kano model is meant to help a company recognize the needs that the customer does not talk about so that these needs can become a priority. To get the most out of this analysis, it should be incorporated into the multi-generational project plan for the business. Of course, you must hit the basic needs first, or your customers will be very disappointed, but the company needs to understand that expectations are going to vary over time. For example, Wi-Fi used to be an added bonus, but for many customers, it has become an expected amenity.

Voice of the Customer

Voice of the Customer (VOC) refers to the preferences, expectations, and comments of the customer regarding your service or product. It is a process that a company can use to gather feedback from customers with the ultimate goal of providing them with better-quality services and products. There are two main methods you can use to categorize your customers:

- *Internal customers*: These are the customers who are already in the organization. These can include departments, employees, and management that are found inside the company.
- *External customers*: These are the customers who exist outside of the company. They are the end-users of the services and products, and they have a vested interest in

the company. These can include some people like the shareholders, clients, and the end-users.

The organization must be proactive and innovative all the time to keep up with the changing requirements and needs of their customers. Voice of the Customer can be spoken or unspoken. The VOC methodology is going to be used to capture the customer needs with verbatim comments. Through VOC, the company will be able to translate the comments that the customer gives them into customer needs. Then, they can take that information and use it to make new products and services that their customers will need.

The Categories of VOC

To make things simple, we can separate VOC into four broad classes. These four classes are going to be referred to often as AICP. The four broad classes include the following:

> • *Voice of Associate*: This is the feedback given by the employees.
> • *Voice of Investor*: This is the feedback given by the shareholders and people in management.
> • *Voice of Customer*: This is the feedback from the clients and the end-users.
> • *Voice of Process*: This is feedback received after measuring Critical to Quality and Critical to Process.

VOC Methods

There are a variety of ways you can obtain the feedback you need from your customers. Some of the best techniques to use are as follows:

> • *Direct interviews*: These are one-on-one meetings with potential or existing customers. The interviewer will have questions, and the answers given by the customer will be used to help the company understand what they need to add or improve on.

• *Observations*: This entails watching the behavior or the response of the customer to the products and services.

• *Focus groups*: This involves placing together a group of individuals in one room. They will then be prompted to discuss specific topics that are related to the products or services of the company.

• *Surveys*: These are questionnaires that are to be sent out to the customers. These are pretty popular to use because they are very cost-effective, but those who do often don't get a great response rate from the customers.

• *Suggestions*: The opinions of the customers are collected and then analyzed to see whether they can be used to improve products or services.

In time, you might find that VOC methods are not always the best. Sure, they can give you a great start on understanding what your customers want, but often, the customer will not be able to explain their needs in a way that can help a company improve or create good products and services that the customer actually want. Some of the reasons for this are as follows:

• The customer may not be aware of what the company does.

• The customers are used to showing creativity only when it is their own jobs, not when analyzing the services or products they use.

• Customers can react to a specific idea they hear, but they have great difficulty with coming up with their own ideas.

• Customers can sometimes lie about how much they like a new product. Perhaps they don't want to start an argument or cause offense.

Since asking the customer is not always the best way to help you improve your process or service, you need to find some other way to get the response you want from your customers. And there is! The best way to do this is at the moment is through customer ethnography.

Customer Ethnography

Customer ethnography involves making close observations about your customers and incorporating their behaviors into the design of your service or product. Ethnography is also known as the systematic study of a group of people in their natural setting.

For this to work, a company needs to be able to find a way to integrate itself into the lives of its customers. This helps them have a better understanding of the needs of the customer and of the way their customers use the company's products and services in real life.

Ethnography is meant to help generate a more intuitive understanding of what the customer needs so that you can come up with creative solutions. To do this, the company could start by selecting ten of its potential or existing customers. Ethnography is more concerned with quality rather than quantity, so this number should be enough. The company would then go and hire a team of trained personnel to help observe these customers. The aims here should be the following:

- Establish a full and holistic perspective on the needs of their customers. Every behavior or activity that is in any way associated with a specific need, service, or product will be noted.
- Recognize and note down things that the customer does, especially the actions done subconsciously.
- Identify the frustrations that the customer has and whether these frustrations are linked to the product or not.

As you can see, ethnography has the potential to help an organization develop some really deep insights into the behavior and the needs of their customer. And if it is done properly, it is going to help you make great innovations in the products and services that you provide.

However, ethnography is very time-consuming and labor-intensive. A company also needs to show some caution because they essentially depend on a small sample of their customers as they try to design or improve their products. In the end, when you are done doing your ethnographic study, you should follow up with some traditional VOC methods to help verify your findings.

Understanding how your customer behaves, what some of their basic needs are, and what other things they are looking for can help make a big difference in the types of products that you will design for them. This can help you connect with your customers much better and will ensure that your profits grow in the process.

Chapter 8: How to Get Top Management Support

To get Lean Six Sigma to work, you need to get everyone in the company on board. This means that, before you get started with this program, it is critical that everyone in top management is also completely on board. With that said, however, there are going to be times when the improvement efforts will be driven by mid-level or lower managers rather than those at the top.

In some cases, you may end up with a top management that is not interested in implementing Lean Six Sigma. They may not want to invest the money and the time to do this process when they are already dealing with a lot of other financial pressures. This can make it very difficult for the process improvement measures to spread throughout the whole organization as they should.

The good news is that two different approaches can help turn top management reluctance into support. These approaches are the stealth approach and the limited initial commitment approach. Let's take a look at each of them and see what they can do for you.

Stealth Approach

With this approach, management or individual departments are going to start implementing the methods of Lean Six Sigma, but on a small-scale and under the radar. The aim is to actualize significant benefits of the improvement processes while still maintaining a low profile. Several variations come with this approach, but here are the general techniques you can follow to make it work:

>1. *Identification and clear articulation of the gap that separates your desired process performance and the actual performance*: This can be done with a small core group of those who believe that they need to improve the process. It is recommended that one or more of the core group has some knowledge about Lean Six Sigma.
>2. *Articulation of the needs of your project*: This same group is going to come up with different reasons why the improvements that can come with using Lean Six Sigma are beneficial to the company. This could include customer and financial reasons. They can also include some emotional reasons, such as more pride in the work, getting rid of the bureaucracy, and reduced job frustration.
>3. *Utilization of the project selection criteria to assess potential projects*: These criteria can include a variety of things including a quick payback, business strategy support, higher potential for success, availability of your data, and the self-contained process that won't need help from senior management. The team would also spend some time adding other criteria that can help show how valuable Lean Six Sigma can be to the management.
>4. *Completion of project organization*: The champion level in your team should be selected to help resolve any

political battles that come up. Every team member also needs to receive training to help implement the process.

5. *Addressing the problem with the help of DMAIC*: For this part, your focus needs to be placed on achieving a few quick results rather than sticking with the methodology too much. This means that you would pick out some simple Lean Six Sigma principles and then work only on those. For now, you'll only want to show the senior management the benefit of Lean Six Sigma and then build up from there.

6. *Present the results*: At this point, you would show the results to your top management. After that, your team would request to implement Lean Six Sigma throughout the whole organization.

Limited Initial Commitment Approach

The second approach that you can work on is the limited initial commitment approach. The goal of this approach is to help fix a few problems in the company that are of interest to the top leadership. You also want to be able to demonstrate the improvement quickly. If this is done, it is going to be so much easier for the senior management to commit and agree to a broad rollout of Lean Six Sigma. The steps to use when implementing this approach are as follows:

1. *Engaging with the top management*: You will want to come up with two to four problems that need to be fixed. This team is going to have three core members, and at least one of them has to have some knowledge of Lean Six Sigma.

2. *Collaboratively develop criteria for which project to select*: Pick out three projects that will meet the criteria you've set. Some of the criteria that you may want to consider include readily available data, high potential for success, rapid payback, supporting at least one senior

management problem, and supporting the business strategy.

3. *Finalize the project organization*: In this step, there should be some frontline employees as well as mid-level managers that are involved, and they should have the right training in place.

4. *Identify the stakeholders who are critical*: Your goal is to find ways to get them to commit to the success of your team. This is going to involve your original core group and perhaps 15 or so other people. You would then split them up into a few sub-teams to help out.

5. *Use DMAIC to help address your problem*: Like with the other option, the focus here needs to be on the results, and on getting them quickly, more than on strictly adhering to the methodology. You want to show that Lean Six Sigma can give the company results quickly.

6. *Conduct regular checks to make sure of progress and any financial gains*: If there has been some progress made, there should be celebrations and even gifts of some sort awarded. This will be a step that involves top management as well as the improvement team. The status checks need to be conducted at regular intervals throughout your project.

7. *Presenting your final results*: Show the results to your senior management and use it to convince them to roll out this methodology throughout the whole company.

How to Overcome Any Reluctance to Lean Six Sigma

If you have some people in top management not interested in implementing Lean Six Sigma, there are a few steps that you can use to overcome this reluctance. Some of the things that you should try to include the following:

- *Ensure that the results are fast*: The benefits of your project need to be seen quickly, and they need to exceed any costs that you incur. At a maximum, you should have a timeframe that is no longer than five weeks, and your aim should be a 30% or more return. You want to really turn the heads of the management and show what Lean Six Sigma can do.
- *Use good project selection criteria*: This ensures that your team can pick the best projects and demonstrate as much value as possible to top management.
- *Define the scope of the project well*: The scope needs to be narrow enough that completion can be done fast and broad enough that it can bring in some real benefits. The team members need to be able to keep their eyes fixed on their original project goals to make this happen.
- *Set your own goals*: A team that can set its own goals is one that will find it so much easier to stay committed and motivated to complete the projects – despite the other pressures that they may have.
- *Get experts in Lean Six Sigma*: The team must find people, whether this is externally or internally, who know how to implement Lean Six Sigma and its principles. This will make it more likely that the process is used properly and that it will be implemented throughout the whole company.
- *Monitor the progress*: You want to come up with a plan that has some key milestones, clear deliverables, and responsibility allocations. This will make it more likely that you will get fast and high-quality results. You need to be able to show the management, who might not all be on board, that you can get some great results when you use Lean Six Sigma.
- *Target processes that are people-intensive rather than machine-intensive*: Improvement projects that involve

people tend to bear better results because humans are going to have more variability compared to machines. This means that you are going to get some great innovations that you just can't get when you work with machines.

• *Create a great team atmosphere*: The way that your team members interact with one another will make a big difference in how successful the project is. The leaders of the project must be able to bring their teams together on a regular basis to help improve working relationships.

For Lean Six Sigma to really work for your business, you need to make sure that everyone is on board. It is not enough to just have a few people, or a few departments, understand the value of this method if the rest don't care about it at all. Using some of the strategies in this chapter will help you get the rest of the company and all its management to view Lean Six Sigma with more enthusiasm.

Chapter 9: Deployment Planning

Deploying the process of Lean Six Sigma is going to be a decision that your company needs to take seriously. Tough questions need to be asked as well as answered before you take these critical steps. A good step to start with is to sit down and create a plan that will address the various key issues that affect the processes of your business. The leaders and the executives that help with this project will also need to list out some of the potential challenges that the company may face.

Making the Decision to Deploy

The level of success that you attain with the initiatives of Lean Six Sigma are going to depend on whether or not you meet certain conditions. Before you make this kind of decision, there will be a few questions that you need to ask:

> 1. *Are there compelling reasons for deploying Lean Six Sigma?* Each initiative is going to have some obstacles when you first deploy it. Having a simple and motivating reason to deploy this process will help you break through these obstacles. Some of the compelling reasons could be that there is poor customer satisfaction or that there are new rivals that are starting to dominate the market.
> 2. *What are your explicit goals of the initiative?* Having a burning platform is one of the best ways to develop the push that is required to deploy Lean Six Sigma. However,

there needs to be a pull. The pull will come from your goals, ones that are specific and show you how the company will look in the future. These goals need to highlight the business case for Lean Six Sigma, and they can include the following:

    a. Fundamental changes in the business culture and management

    b. Effective conversion of the strategy into results

    c. Increasing revenues

    d. Reduction of costs while still being able to improve the satisfaction of your customers

    e. Solving problems that are present in the organization

3. *Are those in top management supportive of this initiative?* Leadership is not going to have a substitute. There needs to be involvement to help steer the process, hold the managers accountable, and tear down any barriers that may come up.

4. *Will Lean Six Sigma be able to resolve any of the problems that are bothering the organization?* Most organizations believe that this process is going to be able to solve all their problems. While this process is great, it isn't the answer to everything. For example, if the company has bad leadership, poor business strategy, and financial restructuring, then Lean Six Sigma is not going to offer the appropriate solutions. You have to look through your business and determine whether this is the best option for you or not.

Choosing a Good Deployment Model

This deployment model refers to the focus, scope, scale, and structure of your deployment. There are going to be many models that you can use, but you will want to make sure that the model you choose is right for your organization. There are four models that you can use for deployment:

Organization-wide Model

This is seen as the traditional model that most organizations use. It is going to require strong management that the top leaders should drive. Every sector of this organization is involved, and the results are felt quickly. This method will allow you to improve more than one function at a time since they are all involved. The obstacles that come with deployment are going to be broken down with the help of top management.

The biggest problem with this model is that you must have good leadership to make it work. This can be a big issue for some businesses. There also needs to be a committed deployment team. This model is going to use a lot of resources and, in some cases, there are other initiatives in the company that could suffer. It can be difficult to execute correctly as well. However, if done properly, it can have a big impact on the business. This model is considered to be the most sustainable.

Business Unit Model

With this model, you will deploy Lean Six Sigma with just one of the units or departments of your business. It is going to be less complex compared to the previous model because you will only need a small part of your company to support the various functions like project monitoring and training. Because it is smaller in size and nature, it is sometimes easier to get management to adopt these ideas. It will still need a strong department leader, but it won't need executive support at the beginning, which makes it a good fit for companies whose people may be skeptical about using Lean Six Sigma.

The disadvantage of using the business unit model is that it is not going to have a big impact on the culture of the company. It is also going to be difficult for the deployment team to work across the departments to help improve them. This model will need to prove itself first before you can move it over to the whole company, and this can take years.

Targeted Model

With the targeted model, the Lean Six Sigma method is going to be deployed to attack a specific problem that exists either inside one department or in the whole organization. The implementation is going to be fast and effective. Due to the limited scale of this initiative, you do not need a ton of infrastructure, and you do not need to make a lot of changes. The problems can be the focal point and the motivation to take action. This model is sometimes a good way to show how effective Lean Six Sigma quickly.

On the other hand, this model is narrowly focused, and it won't be able to transform the business. Additionally, since there isn't a lot of infrastructure in place to help support the model, it can become difficult to expand this initiative to other parts of the organization should you decide to.

Grassroots Model

This method involves a few individuals in the lower ranks of the company deploying Lean Six Sigma to solve a problem. There is not going to be much infrastructure to support this one because of its scale, so it is pretty easy to implement. If the localized initiative is successful, it is possible for other departments to become interested in this method as well.

The problem that comes with this model is that it rarely ever turns into a broader deployment. It is more of a guerilla style of deployment where the top level of management is not going to be involved, and thus, most of the resources that are needed will not be there. Since there isn't a lot of support, it is hard to expand the narrow scope later on. With this model, the results that you obtain are going to be very small for the whole company, and they are less likely to capture a lot of attention from top management.

Getting the Right Talent

The culture of your company can sometimes be changed by taking on a few high-potential employees, spending some time to train them as Black Belts, and then putting them back into the workforce in a leadership position. These employees can then work on applying the principles of Lean Six Sigma each day.

The challenge for most companies is identifying whom the high-potential employees are, figuring out how to position them in the right leadership posts, and then managing the expectations and perceptions of others in the company. There is also a little fear that rival companies will poach the employees who are recognized as the top performers. In addition, the managers can have differing opinions about who is a top performer. Working with the HR department and crafting good policies can make a difference when trying to make this work.

Maintaining Focus

Many initiatives are going to struggle with focusing on the issues that matter the most. Think of a team that completes these improvement processes only to learn that no one cared about the problem in the first place. Irrelevance is the greatest threat to a Lean Six Sigma initiative.

The plan's deployment should always place its emphasis on the issues that are relevant. Management should never focus their attention on any project that is irrelevant, mediocre, or small simply to make sure that their Black Belts are busy. And to make sure that Lean Six Sigma stays relevant, the right projects must be selected. To figure out which projects are the most relevant the top business goals should be taken into account.

It Is Worth It?

Your organization is going to get some great results when it deploys Lean Six Sigma. There are going to be some risks, but they are not technical. The methodology, tools, and training are not complex enough to justify putting off the initiative. What ultimately makes the difference between an impactful deployment and a failed management initiative is the ability to sort out issues of change management, leadership commitment, talent management, and accountability for results.

Deployment Mistakes Your Business Should Avoid

By this point, you should know that deploying Lean Six Sigma is going to produce a ton of benefits for your business. However, it is possible that the Lean deployment will end up failing when you get started, which can result in wasted time and resources. This is often because the deployment mistakes weren't handled the way they should have been. It is important that you recognize these mistakes and learn to avoid them at all costs. Let's look at some of the most common Lean Six Sigma deployment mistakes that you should avoid and how to resolve them.

Weak Leadership Support

The main way that you are going to get some success with Lean Six Sigma is to bring on some strong leadership commitment. The top management needs to be supportive of the project you want to implement throughout the company, and they need to take actions to help back up their words.

The solution is to keep the top leadership engaged in all steps of the process. Senior management needs to take their time to communicate the right way with the staff, stressing how important it is to focus on the Lean Six Sigma project as the way to achieve organizational objectives. The leadership also needs to allocate some time to review deployment progress to make sure that things are on track during all management meetings.

Too Broad of a Scope

Whenever your Lean Six Sigma project ends up failing, it would usually be due to scope creep. If your scope is too broad when you start, this could lead to you not having enough focus to guarantee the improvement of a product, service, or process. There are times when your scope will increase right in the middle of the project. To avoid this issue, the team needs to concentrate on maintaining a narrow scope so that you don't end up biting off more than you can chew.

Poor Deployment Strategy

The aim of having this deployment strategy is to ensure that your company goals stay aligned with some of the deployment outcomes that you have. If there isn't alignment, the stakeholders are going to fail to see what the point of the entire process is. The best solution to this kind of problem is to make sure that your business goals and your deployment results are aligned.

The deployment strategy must always take into account project execution, employee training, account planning, information management, and the achievement of operational excellence. There also needs to be periodic reviews of the progress that you are making with each strategy and how it is impacting business results.

When you can monitor these elements, the team is better able to perform any of the necessary adjustments. When there are positive changes that people can see, the organization will start to gain more belief in the effort.

Too Much Emphasis on Training and Certification

For some companies, it is easy to fall for the idea that every person who has some kind of involvement in the Lean Six Sigma project needs to know all the details about the tools and the techniques that will be used. Of course, there is a lot of different certification and training courses out there, and there are even trainers and consultants who will compete heavily to corner the market.

Because of all this, you will find that there is a ton of focus on teaching advanced tools to employees and getting them certified. The truth here is that not every Lean Six Sigma tool needs to be used in every project. The solution here is to place more emphasis on learning expediency and the application of knowledge. There are times when you'll need to have individuals trained in Lean Six Sigma, but you don't need to teach everyone in your company. Your company needs to stay focused on executing your projects rather than on how many certified Belts there are.

Poor Project Selection

One of the most important decisions that you can make when it comes to the Lean Six Sigma process is selecting which project you want to work with. If your project improvement team ends up losing focus in the beginning and they don't do a good job of selecting as well as prioritizing projects, disaster is going to strike. When the wrong project is chosen, it can lead to the whole project being scrapped or delayed, possibly causing cynicism among the Belts.

The best solution for this is to make sure that the goals and the data are the key elements that you and your team focus on when you are selecting your projects. There need to be meetings put together to help review data, the customers, as well as the process and business goals. The team should also take the time to make sure that each project the company selects has a sponsor who is in charge of monitoring that project and giving the approval necessary.

Not Picking Out a Deployment Leader

Some organizations have tried to deploy a new Lean Six Sigma project without taking the time to designate a deployment leader. Without this leader in place, the teams will engage in the right improvement activities in their own areas, but there won't be unity or synergy of purpose. This is going to lead to failure and confusion within the project.

The solution to this is appointing a deployment leader right from the start. The responsibilities that fall to this leader are to train all the team members, assign the projects, and then select the tools that should be used. The deployment leader is basically the one who is going to provide direction for the project and will ensure that there is some progress.

Isolated Implementation

Think about this: what point is there in improving the design of your product when you choose to leave the manufacturing process as it is? Deploying small localized improvement projects is not a smart strategy. It may be a place for your company to start with if you have limited resources, but you will find that disconnected and isolated pockets of improvements are not going to give you the benefits that you want.

When working with Lean Six Sigma, the best organization results are going to be achieved with the help of adopting a pervasive implementation strategy. After all, a company is made up of processes that are interconnected and work together. If you isolate one of your processes from the others and hope that it all works out, you are going to be disappointed. It's far more likely that the project will fail.

Chapter 10: Project Identification and Selection

Before you start to deploy a Lean Six Sigma project, you must identify and select the right projects. Most companies will do a good job of selecting a bunch of different projects, but they don't have the right techniques in place to help identify the project that is the most relevant and needs to be taken care of first. There are generally going to be four preconditions that you should satisfy to help you identify and select the project to work on using Lean Six Sigma.

Step 1: Understand the Strategic Plan of the Company

The deployment team needs to be familiar with what the company's strategic plan is all about. Strategic planning is going to include some of the following:

- Developing a roadmap to accomplish your strategic plan.
- Evaluating the interest that the stakeholders have.
- Formulating a mission statement after getting some input from the stakeholders.
- Creating a business model that is workable. This step will need to consider a variety of issues, such as financial and cultural ones, that will result from any restructuring

that you do in the current business lines. Adding some new business lines is something that you should consider as well.

- Financial and performance auditing to figure out the capabilities and fiscal muscles of the company.
- Performing a gap analysis to help generate a list of gaps. This process can be done by comparing the performance of the process with what you hoped to achieve.
- Creating and then implementing an action plan that can help you accomplish any of your chosen strategies while also closing up the gaps that are present.
- Developing a plan B, or a contingency plan, that will help deal with potential fluctuations that can happen in the market. You should also consider any pressure you get from the competitors and some other situations that can come up and affect how well you can execute your strategic plan.
- Develop a new plan for the whole company. This could be done when you establish measurable performance indices, cascaded goals, and clear timeframes. The process owners must be identified.

Step 2: Align the Improvement Efforts with the Business Strategy

Your project select team needs to understand how the activities designed for process improvement should align with the strategic action plans. In the first step, the team needs to consider business modeling as a critical aspect of strategic planning. The team would probably spend time analyzing and then identifying the Line of Business and where it is going to fall relative to the company's competitive position and market growth. The objective is for you to find a good and effective strategy for a specific LOB based on your rate of market growth and how competitive the LOB is.

For example, if the LOB of a company has a solid competitive position in the market, this means it is growing well. If this is true, it is best for the company to prioritize their product development instead of improving operations. However, if the LOB has a weak competitive position in a market that is growing slowly, then the company should consider working with Lean Six Sigma to help improve its cost structure.

Step 3: Incorporate the Action Plan into the Policy Deployment System

The policy deployment refers to cascading the goal-based plans through the different levels and departments of the business. Examples of the way that this can be implemented include management by objectives and Hoshin planning. To implement your policy deployment successfully, a few things need to fall into place:

- Use the action plans that were defined in the strategic plan to help you set the right goals, targets, schedules, and owners.
- Work with a cascaded high-level goal to help establish the right goals, targets, schedules, and owners.
- Incorporate these local goals so that you can define the performance plans for both your teams and for the individuals.
- Perform reviews on a regular basis to gauge the performance and the achievement of the high-level goal. This can also be done for the local goals.
- Link the performance of management to help you to establish the right goals when setting up the bonus structure.

Step 4: Recognize the Core Processes of the Business

All companies are going to be engaged in some processes that are designed to transform some type of input into an output that the customer is willing and able to pay for. It is important for the company to clearly define the processes that do this and how they make the customers happy, as well as to have a way to document all of this information.

To help you understand how to examine the performance of processes and then identify the areas that you need to improve, there are a few terms that you should apply:

> • *Level 1 processes*: These are the processes of the business that are considered central to the company. These are going to be linked to the function of the business, and you can trace these through accounting records.
> • *Level 2 processes*: These are some of the sub-processes found in level 1. They comprise a series of process steps that are related.
> • *Work steps*: This is the work unit that can fall under a level 2 process. It comprises a series of tasks that are performed by either a small team or by an individual.

The most effective way to determine the opportunities that you need to improve is first to recognize the processes that will fall to level 1. These can then be broken down so that the critical level 2 processes are revealed. Once this is accomplished, you can implement Lean Six Sigma to help fix any problems in the work steps.

Identifying, Prioritizing, and Selecting Projects

There is going to be a structured methodology that the Champions, Master Black Belts, and Black Belts will need to follow to help them identify, prioritize, and "cheese" the projects they are going to work on. In the beginning stages, the Champion is responsible for helping a trained Master Black Belt undertake the following steps:

- Review the strategic plan
- Understand the goals and objectives of the company
- Conduct a comparison between the performance that is desired by the company and the way that the company is actually performing
- Understanding the goals that occur in each department and the objectives for every business function
- Conduct a comparison between the desired performance that you want to achieve and the actual performance; this needs to be done for each business function
- Identify the core level 1 processes; you can do this by looking at an analysis of the goals, returns, and risks of each one
- Do the same thing with the level 2 processes
- Brainstorm all the potential opportunities that you can have for improvement
- Take the time to rank and prioritize all the potential opportunities for improvement according to their goals, returns, and risks
- Communicate the outcome of this ranking process; you can talk about it with the team and then come up with a consensus about what everyone wants to pursue. If there are some who dissent a little bit, it is important to discuss this ahead of time and make sure you are on the same page
- Launch the Lean Six Sigma project. These should be done according to the schedule that you established prior

The Champion, the Master Black Belts, and the Black Belts, along with everyone else in the company, need to work together to finish this part. It is not going to work if only a few select people in the business agree to the project and the rest just go along for the ride without understanding their roles or having any desire to see Lean Six Sigma and its projects do well in the long run.

In addition, the project that you pick needs to be very important to the company. You can see some amazing results when working with Lean Six Sigma. However, if you waste your time picking out some small projects that don't amount to much, you are wasting a lot of time and resources, and even money, in the process. Take a look at the business model and strategy, decide which projects need to be done, and then go with the one that is going to provide you with the best benefits and the most return on investment.

Chapter 11: How to Select a Viable DMAIC Project

One of the most important components that you have to consider when it comes to whether or not a project will be successful is selecting the right projects. In cases where the practitioner is going to be lax about selecting the opportunities for improvement, the end results are going to be pretty disastrous. It is not good enough to just choose a project based on how easy it is to complete or on a few obvious inputs. This is the low-hanging fruit, and while it can work sometimes, it is not supposed to be the main criteria to help you define the approach that you will use. This is especially true when the priorities you set are not clear.

There needs to be a consistent approach in play that will help you figure out whether or not your project will be a good DMAIC project while also helping you to prioritize the projects according to the resources allocated. To make this happen, there must be certain selection criteria in place.

Critical Project Criteria

Different criteria must be in place before you get started with your Lean Six Sigma project, and these will help ensure success. Some of the criteria include the following:

- *Customer impact*: You must determine whether the success of the project is going to make a big difference in the way both external and internal customers perceive the quality of the product or service. You can use a VOC analysis to help with this.
- *Service quality impact*: You must determine if the service quality will be enhanced through the value chain. Though the customer may be satisfied, you could find that this is useless if the process ended up being too complex or difficult to implement consistently.
- *Defect definition*: The process defect needs to be defined so that the team doesn't start to lose focus and become more affected by scope creep. The final output should not be what you use to measure the defect. For example, failure to achieve your revenue targets can be a high-level problem, but it should still not be used as your defect metric. The defect metric must be an operational aspect, such as rework rates, lead times, and cycle times.
- *Process stability*: Before you improve a process, you need to check for stability. Stability doesn't mean that you have reached your desired performance. An unstable process can generate noise that may interfere with the accurate assessment of how impactful the improvements are.
- *Availability of data*: There needs to be some data available to help you study a process and decide whether or not you should improve it. If you do not have this data available, you must attain it. You need to make sure that

you can get your key data without using a ton of resources.

• *Availability of your dedicated team*: The company is going to need both Black Belts and Green Belts to keep the momentum going. Remember that your team members may sometimes have other functions to perform each day so you will have to account for how much time they can spend on this project.

• *Benefits*: Any potential project you choose to go with must be analyzed to find out the value it can provide. This is possible with a discounted cash flow model. There is also a necessity to include some soft benefits. This includes things like customer satisfaction and the impact it has on sales and retention.

• *Clarity of the solution*: If the solution to your problem is already clear, you do not need to waste your time with the DMAIC process. However, it is possible that there are many good solutions that you are floating around, and you may want to look for some root causes rather than just rushing in and trying to fix the symptoms.

• *Project sponsorship*: You must have everyone on board with the same project. This will make a difference on whether the project is successful or not. Without this, the fate of the project could end up hanging in the balance.

• *Project timeline*: One of the benchmarks you can use to determine how reasonably fast you can finish a project is the six-month mark. The viability of a DMAIC project is judged on whether it can be completed in this timeframe or not. If not, then the feasibility of the project diminishes. When picking out a project, take the time to look through it and see how long it will take to hit all of the milestones. You want to see results quickly when you are working with the Lean Six Sigma process, so make sure that the timeline is optimal.

- *Project alignment*: The project needs to align with the strategic goals of the company. If it doesn't, the top management is going to be much more reluctant to authorize, much less finance, it.
- *The probability of implementation*: Here you will ask the question "What are the chances of the solution being implemented in the organization?" The organizational changes, adjustment of goals, rival initiatives, and resistance levels are all going to be factors that you should assess to determine the probability of the solution being implemented.
- *Control over the inputs*: Once some of the data that you need is collected, the team will then evaluate if there are enough inputs that you can control and measure. If it is not possible to have some reasonable control over the inputs of the process, it becomes so much more difficult for you to achieve your objectives.
- *Investment*: You can ask here how much money it will cost to fix whatever the problem is. If the project needs a large amount of capital to implement and that capital is hard to regain, it is not really a good idea to go ahead with it. Plus, if you have a project like this, it is automatically not going to satisfy the requirements of a good Lean Six Sigma improvement project and should therefore not be done.

When you are working on a Lean Six Sigma project, it is imperative that you identify and select the right project and that the right people are in charge of deploying it. If the company uses the right criteria throughout the whole undertaking, they are going to increase their chances of making the project successful.

Chapter 12: Value Addition and Waste

In business, there is going to be a value-added process. These are a series of activities that your company can use to meet the following criteria:

- The activities need to make a difference or effect changes in the product or service.
- The customer must still be willing to pay for the output of the process.
- The process activities need to be performed correctly the first time around.

Applying Wastes to Transactional Processes

The eight wastes discussed in Chapter 2 that constitute the acronym DOWNTIME can be used in manufacturing as well as in some transactional processes. However, when it comes to these transactions, wastes can be applied more simply and logically. For example, let's assume that there are two departments involved in these processes, with an activity that is conducted by Department A ending up being reworked by Department B. A team is in charge of improving the process so that they can eliminate waste. The team will examine the current process and will come up with the following questions:

> • *Were all the process activities that we have performed done in a consistent, correct, and sequential manner? Does each of these activities add value?* If an activity doesn't add some value, it shouldn't be used.
>
> • *Have the interfaces between and within the departments been defined and are they working? Is it clear who owns each interface?*
>
> • *Are the decision-making criteria clear and understood by everyone? Are there any dangling process steps?* Some steps will lead nowhere. This happens when there isn't a process output or a clear customer output.
>
> • *Does the process require any type of rework to fix defects? Where do the defects originate?* Answering these can help you find the defects. If there is no process in place to rework any of the defects, then you can take the time to create a strategy to create one for your business.

The above questions are important because they can help practitioners improve their process. You need to go through your company and see if any of the DOWNTIME wastes are present. They cost you time, resources, and money. Lean Six Sigma can help you get rid of these wastes, and asking the questions provided can help you spot them easier.

Examples of Waste Problems

Problem 1: The activity wasn't performed accurately or consistently

The first problem we will discuss is when an activity isn't performed in the right manner. Let's take a look at a scenario about how this can happen in a company. According to how a company is supposed to process payments, customers should have their payments matched to the right account before the next billing cycle. However, about ten percent of the time, this might not be possible. This means that the funds are going to go into a suspended account. The company would then need to get a good team together who would spend their whole time investigating the suspended payments rather than doing their other work.

During this time, the process would be mapped out, and then the team would discover that there were ten methods they could use to resolve the issue. The solutions will then be explored, and they'll find that the methods they currently have in effect are inefficient. The improvement team then would go through the solutions they've come up with and pick out the best one.

After picking out the best solution, the company would be in charge of training employees on the new method they need to use. The company would then be able to reduce the number of staff that investigated the suspended payment by half.

Improvement actions: The guidance, as well as the work instructions, will be provided, and the personnel who will be trained will then be held accountable for their actions.

Problem 2: The activity wasn't performed in the right sequence

Sometimes, the work is going to get out of order, and that can mess up the production process and make it hard to get things done efficiently and cost-effectively. Let's look at another scenario for this one. In most companies, an employee will be required to have an ID badge to be shown to the right people when they come inside the building. In some places, they would also use these badges to access the computers within their company. Though there is similar information that the computer should be scanning for in the two processes, they are often going to be viewed as distinct processes.

When the company sees these as different processes, the company will lose a lot of productivity. This often happens with new recruits or with individuals who are transferred to a different department.

The company will need to decide that it is much better to combine these two ID requirements and then instruct the new employees on how they should comply. Before they are implemented, the HR will need to spend time checking to see that all the security information has been uploaded. When the new employees arrive to work that day, they will be sent straight to the security departments and to IT to help begin the process for an ID.

When the new employees have received their ID from the security and IT departments, they will then be sent over to sign up with payroll. When all of this information is set up and ready to go, the employee will then receive their new badge.

Improvement action: This is when the company changed up the sequence of activities. This ensures that things are going to happen in the most efficient manner possible and can prevent any loss of time or other issues along the way.

Problem 3: The loan application process takes too much time

Let's say that a financial institution is in charge of helping get loan applications processed. They find that it is going to take about 21 days to get that loan application approved. This is because the application form for the loan needs to go to a variety of departments to be approved.

When an improvement team was invited to look things over, they tracked one of the documents for the loan process and found that it traveled all throughout the building. They then measured the linear distance that the document traveled and found that overall, it traveled 5,000 feet. The team decided that it needed to isolate all of the relevant departments around one area of the building. This helped reduce 4,800 feet out of the distance the paper needed to travel and cut the approval period for the loan down to just three days.

Improvement action: This step had the company eliminating some of the biggest steps that were not adding value to the process.

Problem 4: Inoperable interface

For this one, there was a team who was given the task of improving the process of scanning documents, and their goal was to minimize the costs from doing this. After some research, the team found that one of the feeders for the documents can store all the relevant information being scanned in an electronic form. Despite this, the organization was still requiring that these documents be printed out before being sent to the scanning department.

This led to several problems for the company. First, it led to a very large surge in the workload for the scanning department. They had to handle all of the work for everyone and were always running behind, making it hard for other departments to keep to their schedules as well. The company also spent a ton of money on paper, and its continued use increases the carbon footprint of the company as well. Overall, this indicated that the company had failed to map out the whole scanning process from start to finish.

Improvement actions: This is where you want to find a clear definition of the interface and then assign accountability and ownership.

Problem 5: Improve processes for making decisions

There will be times when an organization fails to clearly define the decision criteria that should be used in a transactional process. This can sometimes lead to a variation in how your employees will interpret the policies that you have.

For this scenario, an improvement team came in, and they reviewed the auditing process for a mortgage company. This team then found out that different auditors were using different criteria to approve mortgages. In addition, the underwriters were using diverse criteria as well. The result of all this is that some of the people who shouldn't have been approved for a loan were approved and some of those who should have been approved ended up being declined. This was also a root cause as to why so much time was being wasted when it came time to reconcile auditing results.

The improvement team decided to review the risk models and credit policies of the company so that they could come up with some terms that were clearly defined and that everyone could follow. All the underwriters were then trained to follow these rules, and random analysis checks were conducted to ensure that there was more consistency in the decision-making that went on in that mortgage company.

Improvement actions: Clarification of operational definitions, training of employees, and reviewing the decisions.

Problem 6: Processes that are redundant

These are any processes that may have held some value in the distant past but do not need to be used any longer. Since they have been in place for such a long time, however, nobody in the company even noticed that these processes were no longer adding value for them.

This is why it is important for the Lean Six Sigma Belts to go through and challenge the status quo. This allows them to eliminate some of the processes in place that aren't leading them anywhere. For example, many organizations have a system where expense reports are approved by several departments instead of just one. This can cause delays that are not necessary, and that can breed mistrust.

Improvement action: It is the job of the company to eliminate the redundant steps still existing in their processes.

Problem 7: The rework loop

There are many cases wherein rework needs to be done in a transactional process. For example, let's say there's one department in charge of preparing an official document before sending them over to another department. Then, the receiving department finds out that the documents were not filled out properly. This will force the receiving department to stop other work so that they can fix these issues. Before long, this can become a big institutional problem.

The rework loop can be fixed, but you must change some of the culture of your company. Employees need to be trained so that they can take responsibility for the quality of work that they provide rather than having other people check it over and catch mistakes for them.

Improvement action: For this one, you need to identify the root causes of rework, eliminate them, and then track the changes.

Chapter 13: The Process-Improvement Team

Many managers will find that improving the processes of the business is very rarely an easy undertaking. There are going to be different responsibilities that they need to take care of all the time, not to mention the fires that will need to be put out. The resources to implement and improve the business can often be lacking at times, making the job of the manager that much more difficult. While there are going to be numerous obstacles that can make it hard to deploy Lean Six Sigma effectively, there is still one way to leverage the available resources that you have and apply the methodology: assembling a cross-function improvement team.

This team should be made up of a group of people inside the business who are handpicked with the goal of improving a process in mind. The responsibility of putting the team together and managing it will be on the process owner and team leader, and the senior manager will sponsor it.

On the other hand, some organizations decide to go with a process known as a management-led initiative. This is where the managers will start the improvement process on their own. They are going to meet and discuss issues regarding cost reduction and process improvement. Once they have their ideas, the management will then communicate the improvements that they want to implement throughout the organization. This means that the recommendations will trickle downwards with the supervisors policing the initiative and the workers going through and executing the orders.

The Disadvantage of the Management-led Process

Compared to a process that is led by a team, there are many weaknesses inherent to the management-led process. Some of the disadvantages of working with this type of process are as follows:

- The managers in charge of brainstorming and coming up with solutions are typically the ones who are not directly involved in the processes they are trying to fix. This means that they are more likely to address perceived issues rather than the actual ones.
- Since the responsibility for its success will be placed on the supervisors and the management, they are going to be given an even bigger workload.
- The frontline management and the workforce are going to be ignored, and they won't really feel any sense of ownership of the initiative. This is going to mean that most of the people in the business are not going to have any enthusiasm for the project's success.
- Information is going to start with the senior management and then move down throughout the business. This can sometimes lead to miscommunication and confusion.

The Benefits of the Team-led Process

It is often better to go with a process led by a team when working on a Lean Six Sigma project. Some of the benefits of sticking with a team-led approach include the following:

- The people who come up with solutions and ideas for improvements are also the ones who work with the processes on a daily basis. They have a vested interest in resolving the issues, and they know how the processes work so it should be expected that they can come up with the best solutions.

- The ideas formulated are going to move from the bottom up. This can make the frontline staff feel like they are a part of the process. This is a great way to make the whole team more enthusiastic about the initiative.
- It emphasizes teamwork and is going to make your workforce feel like they are appreciated.
- The team will be better able to recognize solutions that they can easily implement. This can save the organization a lot of money, and it will show right away that Lean Six Sigma is improving the process.

How to Create a Winning Team

Now that we have given you some ideas about which type of process is going to be a better fit for you when working on Lean Six Sigma, it is time to look at some of the requirements for creating a good team. For a team to be successful, it is important that they have a good structure and composition. A few important things to remember about building your team are as follows:

- The team needs to have people who know the processes of the business well, as well as individuals with diverse thinking styles. You should include a mix of different people with different jobs, e.g., some process experts along with customers and suppliers.
- The team must appoint a team leader. This leader needs to have a good understanding of the process and at least a bit of experience with project management. They should also know something about applying Lean Six Sigma, as well as be familiar with the tools they can work with. Choose someone who is trained as a Green Belt.

- The team should be a manageable size. Ideally, you should try to keep the team to eight or fewer members to ensure that everyone can participate.
- Meeting times need to be established. The times should work for all so that everyone can attend.
- The first meeting should allow the team to establish their ground rules. All the members need to be informed about what they are expected to do in terms of participation and attendance.
- There should also be someone to serve as the team record-keeper. The job is to write down any good idea that the members come up with.

In addition to the points above, you'll also want to make sure that your team is diverse and include people who are trained in Lean Six Sigma. Having Champions, Master Black Belts, Black Belts, and Green Belts in place will ensure that you are using all the tools that this philosophy has on offer properly. You should consider training the team to attain these belts to further increase your chance of success.

How to Select Your Lean Six Sigma Candidates

If you are planning to get started on a Lean Six Sigma project to facilitate improvement to your business and receive great results, it is critical for you to select the right candidates to help you get the project done. Picking out the right candidates can make or break your whole project. Don't just choose someone because they are in your business or because you want to get the project done quickly. Pick them out because they will provide the best benefits necessary for your project.

What this means is that the Black Belts and Green Belts you choose will need to have all the required traits before you start the program. If they don't, you need to make sure they are trained properly ahead of time or else find someone who already has the right kind of training to help out. The guidelines can be of great help for when you are choosing, and for when it is time to elevate a Green Belt to a Black Belt status.

Green Belt candidates

The first thing to look into is the Green Belts you want to work with. These candidates need to show that they are proficient in starting and finishing projects while also solving problems with the help of a data-based approach. Some of the traits that you should look for in your Green Belts include the following:

- *Interest in Lean Six Sigma*: Your Green Belt must have an interest in improving the processes in your business that are already in existence. This will be evident in their participation in any improvement projects you use. You can also check their track record for quality work.
- *Process orientation*: Your Green Belt needs to be able to visualize the entire process and how the different components interact to produce the output that you want.
- *Knowledge of the process*: It is really important that they understand how a particular project can impact the whole company.
- *Passion*: Your Green Belt candidate needs to show that they are excited and dedicated to being a part of your project.
- *Enthusiasm to learn*: Your Green Belt should be able to learn about different techniques and tools. These should be practiced not only during their training hours but also afterward. This will only happen if the individual has the zeal to learn.

Black Belt candidates

This role is going to place some more emphasis on leadership qualities, which makes it a bit different from the traits that you will find with a Green Belt. You will find that your middle managers will often be good Black Belts. These individuals will need to require all of the same traits that the Green Belts did before, but they also need to satisfy the following criteria:

- *Possess technical skills*: This is going to be a critical factor because your candidate will need to be able to apply some higher-level technical skills during their projects.
- *Have some business acumen*: As the leader of the project, a Black Belt needs to be knowledgeable about the current market that your business exists in. They should also be able to identify the daily challenges of this business. This will help them push your program in the right direction.
- *Have an influential personality*: Your Black Belt must be able to lead. This means that they can help your company to implement the right change, be able to communicate well with different levels of management and be able to give direction to others.
- *Possess problem-solving skills*: A Black Belt must be able to prove their data analysis skills with some of their past projects.
- *Have an attitude towards mentorship*: A Black Belt is the one who is going to be responsible when it's time to train and mentor Green Belts on the team. They will need to provide some expertise to the program and then eliminate any obstacles that could potentially get in the way. In some instances, they may need to conduct some training to help with awareness with Lean Six Sigma.

The Process Owner

Another person we need to talk about with your Lean Six Sigma project is the process owner. This is going to be the person in charge of figuring out how a specific process runs. They are also responsible for ensuring that the process continues to satisfy the customer and the needs of the business for many years to come. Every company that wants to ensure that Lean Six Sigma keeps gaining momentum will need to recognize the role of a process owner. Some of the responsibilities that come with the process owner are as follows:

- They need to understand all the critical parts of the process. This individual will know the elements of the output that both the business and the customers are going to value the most. They must also have a good understanding of how their process is going to align with company goals.
- They are going to track the performance of a process with the help of data. The data used will need to be input metrics as well as some output measures. These input metrics are going to be useful because they will help predict performance from an early stage. In most cases, the process owner will track data that are already compiled by other process operators.
- They are going to ensure that the process is always documented and that this documentation is standardized and updated as often as possible. A company must strive to reduce their variations as much as possible when it comes to the way that employees operate a process. The process owner is going to be responsible for identifying the best practices and then standardizing them to guarantee they get the right quality in the end.
- They establish a process management plan so that everyone who is working on the process can see it. This plan is also going to contain a response plan in case there are signs of trouble around.
- They are going to hold reviews on a regular basis. These are going to include process reviews. During these process reviews, questions are going to be asked regarding things like customer satisfaction, control of

input and output metrics, and who is assigned to deal with any of the various problems that may come up. Another review is the process management review. This is where questions are asked to determine how effective the managing methods and process monitoring methods are.

- They are in charge of ensuring that all the solutions the improvement team identifies are integrated and sustained in the process.
- They are going to ensure that the process operators are well-trained. They also need to make sure that these operators have the right resources and tools to perform their duties as efficiently as possible.
- They will provide a very important link between this process and the customers. The process owner must make sure that he or she is always connected to everyone else in the organization, whether internally or externally.

The role that your process owner plays may seem kind of boring and easy to do, but it is still important to the company. These owners are not going to work alone because there are often many process operators working under them to make following the process easier. However, when the day is done, the process owner will be the one who actually has the power to make any decisions regarding this process.

Chapter 14: Design for Lean Six Sigma

When one hears that a business is using Lean Six Sigma, the assumption is that the methodology they are using is DMAIC. This is often true because the organization will likely be trying to sort through some of their existing processes to single out those that are generating waste. However, there is a second approach that you can use. This is the one companies will implement when they are trying to design a new process or product, and they want a good way to ensure that it meets high-quality standards. This approach is called Design for Six Sigma, or DFSS.

Design for Six Sigma

This is an emergent approach whose main objective is to create a new service or product that doesn't have any defects while also ensuring that the Lean Six Sigma methodology is implemented correctly from the beginning. Design for Six Sigma enables a company to enhance the rate as well as the quality of its design process.

You will find that the approach used for DFSS has major differences compared with DMAIC. For one, the phases of DFSS have not yet been universally defined, and most companies work on their own variations to implement it. This allows a business to tailor DFSS to fit their cultural, industrial, or business needs. If the company decides to hire the services of a consulting company to help, they would simply need to adopt whatever version of DFSS that the consultant recommends. This is why DFSS is considered to be more of an approach that companies can use rather than a distinct methodology.

Design for Six Sigma can be implemented when you are designing or redesigning a product or service, and you want to start from scratch. When the service or product is designed with the help of DFSS, it can be expected that the result would be a Sigma level of 4.5 or higher. What this means is that there will not be more than one defect in every 1,000 opportunities. However, depending on the product, there are times when the Sigma level can be as high as six, but aiming for that can prove to be difficult.

Design for Six Sigma Methodology

The first step to using the DFSS methodology is to identify and then analyze the gaps that are present as they are bound to affect the performance of the new process, product, or service in a negative manner. The main thought to focus on here is how the customer would respond to your new item. If you have that information, you can establish a project that can weather any problems.

There are a few variations you can use with the DFSS approach. These can differ from each other, but they are going to follow steps that are similar, and their ultimate objectives are the same. These DFSS approaches are a way for you to design processes, products, and services that are geared to minimize development costs and delivery time, improve effectiveness, and enhance customer satisfaction. While there are a variety of approaches to use, the basic procedures are as follows:

- Capturing the requirements of the customer
- Analyzing and prioritizing the requirements
- Developing the design
- Tracking the capability of the process, product, or service at every step
- Exposing the gaps between customer requirements and product capabilities
- Establishing a plan for control

How to Implement Design for Six Sigma

Most organizations that implement DFSS tend to focus too much on financial accountability at the expense of implementation accountability. It is important that the company when they choose to implement this, place emphasis on staying as true as possible to the DFSS process. This should be translated into the disciplined and thorough application of the different tools for DFSS, such as transfer functions, expected value analysis, QFD, and more.

When you are ready to get started on implementing DFSS, the company needs to believe that the powerful tools it provides will bring the results they want. However, some signs can show ahead of time whether a company is reluctant to implement DFSS but still expect to get the savings and the benefits. This fear of putting in some hard work is what partly leads the companies that use DFSS to take shortcuts, and these cause them more harm than good.

First, understand why you want to implement with DFSS. Why choose this process instead of sticking with what you already have? To help you find answers, here are some of the benefits you can expect from implementing DFSS:

- It has been proven to provide a gain of at least one sigma quality level compared to some of the other designs.

- It can reduce the time it takes to get your product or your service on the market.
- It can be applied to your business, no matter the type of service, product, or organization.
- It is a very cost-effective way to eliminate defects from a system. The costs of production are going to be the lowest when you are working on the initial phases of your design. This means that DFSS has a high performance-to-cost ratio.
- It can offer you an approach that lends discipline when it comes to accountability of implementation.
- The scorecard enables an enhanced and more consistent collection of the data that you need.
- The DFSS data and the scorecard can help highlight the potential causes of failure. This is better than having to depend on assumptions.

The Basics of Design for Six Sigma

As mentioned previously, there are a few different approaches that you can apply when it comes to making DFSS work. There are some similarities between them, and there are some differences. The good news is that they follow similar steps and can be modified to fit your business better.

You can choose which of the methods to work with. The important thing to remember is that you need to follow all the steps completely and not skip over any of them. Some of the common approaches that you can use with DFSS include the following:

DMADV

While there are different types of approaches that you can go with, the most popular method is the DMADV. Five phases come with this method:

- *Define*: The customer goals, as well as your project goals, should be defined.
- *Measure*: The customer needs and requirements are determined here. The benchmarks that you are going to use in your business are also set.
- *Analyze*: Options are analyzed to help you satisfy the needs of your customers. This is going to require you to truly understand your customer and what they are looking for. It can also help you understand what changes and innovations you can make to a product or service ahead of time so that you can anticipate their needs.
- *Design*: This should detail how the business plans to meet the needs of their customers. This is the plan that you will eventually go through with, but you must have all the details down, along with some explanations, about why a certain step in the plan is important or how it will help.
- *Verify*: Verification is necessary to determine whether the performance can satisfy the customers.

DMADOV

This one is highly similar to the DMADV methodology, but it has another step: the Optimize phase. Here, you are going to use advanced models and tools to help optimize the performance.

DCCDI

- *Define*: This is where you define your project goals.
- *Customer*: This is when you complete your analysis of the customer's needs.
- *Concept*: This involves the development, review, and the selection of ideas.
- *Design*: This step details how the customer needs as well as the specifications of the business can be met.

- *Implementation*: This phase is when you develop and then commercialize your product or service.

IDOV

This is the methodology most commonly used in the manufacturing business. It can sometimes be modified to work in other industries, but it is going to work the best with industries that focus on manufacturing. Its acronym stands for the following:

- *Identify*: This is where you find the CTQs and the specifications of the customers.
- *Design*: The CTQs of the customer are to be translated into functional needs; this information can also further be used for coming up with potential solutions. The best solution is going to be chosen out of the resulting list.
- *Optimize*: This is when you use advanced tools and models to help you optimize your performance.
- *Validate*: This phase is for ensuring that the design you came up with will satisfy the CTQs of the customer.

DMEDI

- *Define*: This step is for identifying the business' problems along with the desires of your customer. To get started, you're going to require some information from the customers and a solid idea of what people in the industry think about your business.
- *Measure*: This one is going to help you determine the requirements and needs of the customers. You can't have a good idea of where to get started or what kind of processes to implement or change if you aren't clear about the needs of your customers or about what will make things better.

- *Explore*: This is where you analyze the processes of the business. You can then use the resulting information to explore the available options for designs that will meet the needs of your customers.
- *Develop*: This is where you deliver the design that is the most ideal or the most pertinent based on the needs of your customer.
- *Implement*: The new design that you created will be put through simulation tests. The point of this step is to check whether or not the design was successful at meeting the requirements of your customer or if you need to make some changes before bringing the product to market. Make sure to do this step. Forgetting to do it or putting it off could result in you sending off the wrong product and wasting a lot of time and money in the process.

As you can see from the approaches laid out above, DFSS encompasses a wide variety of methodologies. By following any of these methods properly, you will find your business reducing its wastes, increasing its profits, and providing its customer with the exact products and services that they are looking for.

Conclusion

Thank you for making it through to the end of *Lean Six Sigma: The Ultimate Guide to Lean Six Sigma, Lean Enterprise, and Lean Manufacturing, with Tools Included for Increased Efficiency and Higher Customer Satisfaction*. The information provided within these pages has given you all of the tools you need to achieve your goals, whatever they may be.

The next step is to start applying what you've learned to your business. Encourage your team to get copies of this book as well so that you can all learn the benefits of Lean Six Sigma and start making meaningful changes in your organization.

Finally, if you found this book useful in any way, a review on Amazon is always appreciated!

Printed in Great Britain
by Amazon